WATCH ANIMALS GROW

Seal Pups

by Colleen Sexton

BLASTOFF! READERS

BELLWETHER MEDIA · MINNEAPOLIS, MN

Note to Librarians, Teachers, and Parents:

Blastoff! Readers are carefully developed by literacy experts and combine standards-based content with developmentally appropriate text.

Level 1 provides the most support through repetition of high-frequency words, light text, predictable sentence patterns, and strong visual support.

Level 2 offers early readers a bit more challenge through varied simple sentences, increased text load, and less repetition of high-frequency words.

Level 3 advances early-fluent readers toward fluency through increased text and concept load, less reliance on visuals, longer sentences, and more literary language.

Level 4 builds reading stamina by providing more text per page, increased use of punctuation, greater variation in sentence patterns, and increasingly challenging vocabulary.

Level 5 encourages children to move from "learning to read" to "reading to learn" by providing even more text, varied writing styles, and less familiar topics.

Whichever book is right for your reader, Blastoff! Readers are the perfect books to build confidence and encourage a love of reading that will last a lifetime!

This edition first published in 2008 by Bellwether Media.

No part of this publication may be reproduced in whole or in part without written permission of the publisher. For information regarding permission, write to Bellwether Media Inc., Attention: Permissions Department, Post Office Box 19349, Minneapolis, MN 55419.

Library of Congress Cataloging-in-Publication Data
Sexton, Colleen A., 1967–
  Seal pups / by Colleen Sexton.
    p. cm. – (Blastoff! readers: watch animals grow)
Summary: "A basic introduction to seal pups. Simple text and full color photographs. Developed by literacy experts for students in kindergarten through third grade"—Provided by publisher.
  Includes bibliographical references and index.
  ISBN-13: 978-1-60014-171-3 (hardcover : alk. paper)
  ISBN-10: 1-60014-171-4 (hardcover : alk. paper)
  1. Seals (Animals)—Infancy—Juvenile literature. I. Title.

QL737.P63S467 2008
599.79'139–dc22

2007040276

Contents

A female seal
and her pup
sleep on the ice.
Each mother has
only one pup.

A mother and her seal pup learn each other's smell and **voice**.

A seal pup flops along on its belly.

A seal pup
is hungry. It cries.
The mother follows
the sound to find
her seal pup.

A seal pup
drinks milk from
its mother.

A seal pup grows **blubber**. This layer of fat keeps the seal pup warm.

A seal pup grows teeth. Now it can eat fish and other ocean animals.

Soon the mother seal will swim away. The pup will follow when it is bigger.

The seal pups **dive** for food. They play in the **ocean** and rest on **shore**.

Glossary

blubber—a thick layer of fat just under the skin; most seals live in cold places and need blubber to keep warm.

dive—to rush head first into the water; seals dive deep and can hold their breath for 20 minutes or longer.

ocean—a large body of salty water; seals live at the edge of the ocean; they live in the water and on the land or ice.

shore—the land along the edge of an ocean, a river, or a lake

voice—sounds made through the mouth; seals bark, snort, moan, and cry.

To Learn More

AT THE LIBRARY

Hewett, Joan. *A Harbor Seal Pup Grows Up*. Minneapolis, Minn.: Lerner, 2001.

Hodgkins, Fran. *The Orphan Seal*. Camden, Maine: Down East Books, 2000.

Kalman, Bobbie. *Seals and Sea Lions*. New York: Crabtree, 2006.

Stille, Darlene. *I Am a Seal: The Life of an Elephant Seal*. Minneapolis, Minn.: Picture Window Books, 2005.

ON THE WEB

Learning more about seal pups is as easy as 1, 2, 3.

1. Go to www.factsurfer.com

2. Enter "seal pups" into search box.

3. Click the "Surf" button and you will see a list of related web sites.

With factsurfer.com, finding more information is just a click away.

Index

The images in this book are reproduced through the courtesy of: Daniel J Cox/Getty Images, front cover; Norbert Rosing/National Geographic/Getty Images, p. 5; Juan Martinez, p. 7; F. Lukasseck/Masterfile, p. 9; Jose Gil, p. 11; Gerry Ellis/Getty Images, p. 13; Norbert Rosing/Getty Images, p. 15; ARCO/De Meester/Age fotostock, p. 17; Richard Bowden, p. 19; kenneth edward lewis/Alamy, p. 21.